Waiting for a Title to Reveal Itself

Guendalina Rota

An imprint of Boom Publications Ltd

272 Bath Street
Glasgow SCOTLAND
G2 4JR

Boom Graduates and the logo are trademarks of Boom Publications Ltd.

Boom Publications Ltd is a more-than-profit company, dedicating over half our profits to university scholarships for underprivileged students worldwide. In order to offset our carbon footprint, we also pledge to plant a tree for each graduation book commissioned.

Waiting for a Title to Reveal Itself
was first published in Great Britain in 2022.

Copyright © Guendalina Rota. Guendalina Rota has asserted her right under the Copyright, Designs and Patents Act, 1988,
to be identified as Author of this work.
For legal purposes any Acknowledgements constitute
an extension of this copyright page.
Cover design by Boom Graduates Ltd and the Book Cover Zone USA.

All rights are reserved. No part of this publication may be reproduced or transmitted in any form or by any means, electronic or mechanical, including photocopying, recording, or any information storage or retrieval system, without prior permission in writing from the publishers.

Boom Publications Ltd do not have any control over, or responsibility for any third-party websites referred to or in this book. All internet addresses given in this book were correct at the time of going to press. The author and publisher regret any inconvenience if addresses have changed or sites have ceased to exist, but can accept no responsibility for any such changes.

Typeset by Helen at Boom Graduates.
Printed and bound in the UK.

To find out more about our authors and books visit www.boomgraduates.com
and sign up for our newsletters.

Waiting for a Title to Reveal Itself

We plant a tree for every
Boom Graduate book commissioned, and
thereafter plant a tree for every 10 books sold.

Watch our forest grow at
https://moretrees.eco/forest/BoomPublicationsLtd/

Guendalina Rota

Waiting for a Title to Reveal Itself

Guendalina Rota

Waiting for a Title to Reveal Itself

Contents

Abstract 9
Preface 11
Introduction 15
Pebbles 23
Water 53
Time 65
Bibliography 71
Author biography 77
Acknowledgements 79
Boom! 81
A note about Boom Graduates 83
Notes 87

Guendalina Rota

Abstract

This book takes into consideration some key concepts of Heidegger's philosophy in the hope of understanding the reason behind the sense of insecurity and incompleteness that accompanies me, as it seems to me that I use my hours in the wrong way and, while I struggle between time and obligations, maybe I am missing something. Why Heidegger? Because his work considers human existence and the idea of man as a thinking being, where meditative thought leads us to have a different and more authentic awareness of our existence. With the metaphor of water that gives shape to pebbles over time, this document collects pebbles of knowledge and explores them in an attempt to understand what causes such uneasiness. The concept of Gelassenheit will be the prevailing one that will lead myself, and perhaps the reader, to learn to wait, freeing themselves from the desire to be in control and opening to what might come. Further comparison to some other work will be made to corroborate the content of some ideas. A wait will follow, once again mimicking the idea of time passing when the water shapes the stones, which hopefully can initiate a new way of thinking and a new awareness of ourselves. Starting with information-rich chapters, which almost leave no room for interpretation, this article will develop at a lighter pace when I consider other works, in which the reader can easily begin his own reflection; then ending with an almost stillness, my personal reflection on the relationship with time and nothing more than a fragment of poetry as a conclusion, hoping to leave a complete openness to the viewer.

Preface

I have no purpose, nor aims.
I do not want to go from "A" to "B", but go together
with all that will come along.
I am open.
I remain still.

Openness and stillness.

In this stillness I am ready to live,
to experience,
to feel
whatever comes.

Guendalina Rota

Waiting for a Title to Reveal Itself

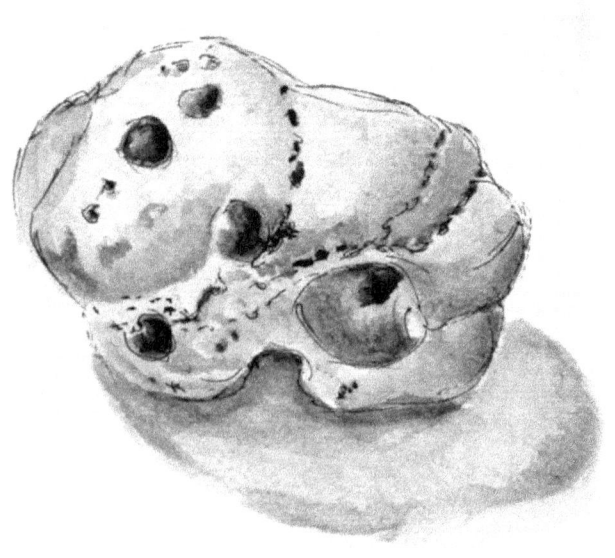

Fig. 1 - Guendalina Rota, *'The gift'*, 2021

Guendalina Rota

Introduction

The primary purpose of this paper is to understand the nature of the feeling of incompleteness and dissatisfaction that dwells in the background of my soul. I will not judge it but simply acknowledge it, I know that it exists, that it is there, and I will not try to fight it, I do not want to eliminate it but to understand it.

In the first section of this article, called 'Pebbles', I will take a journey through some of Heidegger's writings, highlighting those thoughts that come closest to my purpose. It will not therefore be a detailed account but more like a hypothetical walk on the beach where Heidegger's thoughts lie like pebbles and I, from time to time, pause to pick one up because its shape or its colors have caught my attention and I find it beautiful. Why? There is not why, there is not always a need for a why, sometimes it is nice to simply accept what is presented to us, without a specific purpose.

I will start with 'Being and Time', where I will find ideas on the nature of human existence such as the relationship of man with objects, the idea that man chooses what meaning to give to the object he takes into consideration depending on the usage project he has in mind; the idea that the human being is a project of existence, it is potential; the concept of authentic and inauthentic life; the assertion that only death is certain and, with the idea of death in mind, we can live a more authentic life.

The second work of Heidegger that I will consider is 'Memorial Addresses', where the philosopher faces the difficult relationship of strong dependence that exists between the human being and technology, through his concept of calculating and meditative thinking. It explains in a clear and lucid way the risks of the excessive use of technological devices, anticipating modern times in a surprising way, where we find an alienated and ataraxic human being, who no longer stops to understand the true nature of things but accepts the massive quantity of given information in a passive way, by hearsay. Our existence is projected only and exclusively to the ultimate goal, which is profit, monetary or in terms of benefit, without having understood or simply enjoyed the path taken. These considerations are without judgment, it is simply a fact of the current situation, remarkably even if we consider the present day. Yet Heidegger does not say that he rejects technology or that it is bad, on the contrary he understands that it is indispensable and recognizes the benefits of it in our life.

Yet, there is a way to be able to return to having an authentic life, and that is to learn to think contemplatively. Man, by nature, is a thinking being, but he must awaken his capability to a meditative thinking with dedication and constant exercise. Only in this way will human beings be able to use technological devices without being slaves to them, with the power and freedom to be able to detach themselves from them. This freedom from technology is possible if we learn to let go. Heidegger named this ability 'Releasement towards things' and it is another particularly crucial point in his philosophy, together with the openness to the mystery, that is, openness to the hidden nature of things. I will consider how those two concepts are fundamental to explain the meaning of Gelassenheit, that I will explore through the book 'Conversations on the country road' in which, we will see, Heidegger is never clear about this idea because it is impossible to explain with a single word, we will realize that it is more a state of mind, which we can learn with patience and over time.

The understanding of Gelassenheit is what can teach me how to pause and start thinking with no final goal in mind, just for the sake of thinking, freeing myself and opening myself to whatever might come. It tells me, at least, that I have, intrinsic in my being, the ability to think meditatively, which can help me understand the true essence of things, changing my perspective of life, that does not necessarily have to being hectic to be fulfilling.

In the second section of this document, titled "Water", I will find connections between Heidegger's philosophy and some modern works. At this point in my journey, I will have collected some pebbles, now is the time to put them in front of me and understand how they formed over time, thinking about the slow and constant work of water on them. In other words, in my aimless wandering, I will see myself taking into consideration the work of some artists and writers who, in my opinion, reflect the work of Heidegger that, even if in a tangent and non-specific way, like water with pebbles worked through time. Maybe we will not be able to understand in which way it has influenced them, but we can see the results, we can see the smoothness of the pebbles left behind. This means that I will have a different point of view to the information given on Heidegger's key points. Through Marina Abramović, Wolfgang Laib, Basia Ireland, Erling Kagge, Byung-Chul Han, just to name a few, I will try to highlight the points of connection with Heidegger's philosophy. I will not do a detailed and in-depth analysis, but I will simply choose some examples that can corroborate my path.

I hope to be able to argue that Heidegger's philosophy is not obsolete but very relevant nowadays, and it can also help us to understand a different way of living, opening ourselves to things that might happen, my hope is to offer a thought-provoking perspective in which the reader can start his own journey. It is no coincidence that I continue to talk about path and journey, because my investigation is not aimed at a final goal, but open and free to accept what will come, fluid like water.

The last section of this paper is 'Time', where I will sit patiently, and I will wait. It is precisely in this waiting that the thoughts collected so far begin to oscillate and I feel suspended, I let go of wanting to understand, and while waiting, I open to myself. This is one of the aspects of Gelassenheit, here I return to Heidegger and, while waiting, I allow his thought to happen. It is the shortest section of this paper, the most open, the one that needs to be filled in, the one that time will write. It does not matter who fills it, it is there, without judging, it simply exists and waits. I will conclude with a fragment of a poem.

In all three parts of my document, I will choose some images of my artistic practice which are closely related to this path, briefly explaining their meaning. As I have reiterated several times, mine is an evolving, open path, and so is my artistic exploration.

Guendalina Rota

Pebbles

'I am sitting amid this sea of pebbles,

my eyes wander along those colors and shapes,

Maybe I will find 'The' one.

Time is absent.

I stay'

Guendalina Rota, 'Reflections', 2021

As I explained in the introduction, this paper is born from the desire to understand the sense of entrapment and suffocation that has existed, as a background, for much of my adult life and perhaps I have found the right way to make it happen that is, waiting for things to reveal themselves. So, it is not about finding solutions because it would imply that there is a problem while I don't think it is, for me it is a state of mind, a point of view, but there are many ways to understand or see things, and these can change depending on the perspective of the viewer. We can argue that they are all true, especially after encountering some of the points in Heidegger's philosophy, which may have brought me to the right starting point in my understanding which is waiting, since one of the key points is that I do not have to search at all, I just need to wait. But in what way? What does it mean that things reveal themselves? These statements will take on meaning as we delve into this discussion, as I try to highlight those passages or ideas that have helped me open my mind.

Waiting for a Title to Reveal Itself

The rule of things in our ex-sistere.

Shall we start from one of the first works of Heidegger, 'Being and time'? Written in 1926, it is a work in which Heidegger investigates the nature of being from the starting point of being itself. More precisely, Heidegger considers the human being in its ongoing complexity that is: existing in a social dimension, so in relation with others, having emotions that can alter our experience and being aware of death which gives existence a temporality. The human being is not simply considered as an entity that exists, but one that exists there, in that moment and place, and this 'being there' is called Dasein. The question of what being is implies what one asks, of whom one asks and what one finds asking. In this case we ask what being is, to being itself, that is man, and we find the meaning of being in his answer.

> Any inquiry, as an inquiry about something, has that which is asked about [...] has that which is interrogated [...] Furthermore, in what is asked about there lies also that which

is to be found out by the asking [...]. (Heidegger,1962: 4).

Why human beings? Because among all being man is the only being who can ask himself the question about being. A tree does not ask itself what it means to be a tree or what it means to be in general, any more than a bird or a cat does.

The Dasein is the only being that has the possibility to ask the question about being, we are the possibility of existence, projects to be, we are what we choose to be, man is what he decides to be, he is the entity that designs himself. We are projects. Man is beyond mere givenness, he is the architect of his own existence.

If we look at the etymology of the word 'exist' we see that it derives from the Latin ex-sistere, to be beyond, it goes beyond simple reality in the direction of possibility. For Heidegger, man is not simply being but being there, where 'there' is the physical world. Human beings exist in the world, here and now. And since planning is not given to the human being but chosen by the human being himself, the human being goes 'beyond' his own existence, projecting himself into a project. We exist in the world as a project in a transcendent way, and we relate to physical things by taking care of them, and in the way we take care of things we give meaning to things themselves. Man decides how to use things, we have a global vision of things, within which things take on the meaning that man decides.

In summary, the human being, Dasein, finds himself thrown into the world and, in the world, enters into a relationship with things, taking care of them, using them. Things take on a meaning starting from the project, (here we return to the planning of the human being), the project of life that is human being himself and, depending on the project, things take on different meanings. Things therefore have no value in themselves but take on the value of the project in which they are considered.

And how does man create projects? With a usage perspective in mind. Things take on meaning if they are useful for our project. But man is not just a project. We have seen that man is possibility, therefore man is the possibility of projects in the plural. We have more than one way of being in the world, so ours is an open existence. According to Heidegger there are two ways of being open to the world: the first sees us in relationships with things and with others in a functional way, in the second we take care of things and others, our freedom exists if others are also free. But there is more: we can have an authentic or unauthentic existence.

We have seen that man, thrown into the world, is the potential of life and, being the only living creature capable of asking questions about being, he goes beyond mere existence, and plans what will be, that is, start a relationship with things, he takes care of them in the sense that he uses them, he gives them a purpose that will serve his personal project of existence. Heidegger suggests that this kind of existence is not authentic. Man's life plan is anonymous because he accepts things as such, he accepts the facts given without deepening his knowledge of them. But existence in a Western capitalist society, where technology is the driving force behind all things, leads us to come to terms with a vast amount of information that we simply accept without trying to fully understand it, so our existence tends to be not authentic. How come? Since we have moved from real dialogue, where notions and things are questioned, investigated and understood, to the acceptance of chatter, we follow hearsay without going into depth, and thus we give rise to misunderstandings. The quantity and ease of access to anything, allowed by technology, makes us addicted to it: we jump from one thing to another effortlessly, without having to think, it is there ready for us. When we accept everything as given and without thinking, we become a thing between things and our existence, instead of transcending, falls among other things. We fall into a vicious circle of ubiquitous thingness. To rediscover the authenticity of our existence, we must understand our end, death as the only certain thing. It is precisely with the idea of death as absolute certainty that human beings can choose to live authentically, in other words knowing that we are about to die makes a difference in how we live, the authenticity of our existence lies in the way we decide to live, searching for the truth, plunging deeper to discover the very essence of things instead of conforming, appearing, pleasing others and society.

My intention here is not to make a statement on Heidegger's concepts, of which I only skimmed the surface, but to highlight a couple of points that can help me to find or understand what I am looking for. We have seen that man is a potentiality of life, a project of existence, and his is an open existence, because he has multiple possibilities of being. In these concepts I find confirmation of my idea that nothing is defined, fixed, certain, but everything is in motion. Things and places can change meaning and / or purpose depending on the eyes that look at them or the mind that thinks about them, we dwell in uncertainty.

In this regard, I am reminded of an intervention by Professor Tim Ingold, an anthropologist, who, speaking of ice, states that it is not completely solid, rigid, but can break and reconfigure itself. According to Ingold, nothing changes and nothing remains the same, everything flows. The appearance of solid things is always a matter of perceptions and the lifespan of the observer. Although time is a factor taken into consideration, I believe that priority has been given to the way of perceiving things and the possible different points of view. This state of mind, together with the idea that things are in a viscous flow and are never the same, changes the direction of my exploration about the reason of my sense of incompleteness, which is no longer focused on lack of time, but open to understanding other factors. This is reflected in my artistic practice where, while the concept of time remains present, my investigation goes further to understand what lies beyond it.

Perhaps this is where I came up with the idea of holding a clock without hands, made of ice, which slowly melts in this winter weather. The hands have been removed to take away the functionality of the clock as an object and leave only the metaphorical concept of time, which is impossible to hold, to keep, to measure because, before we know it, it has already passed.

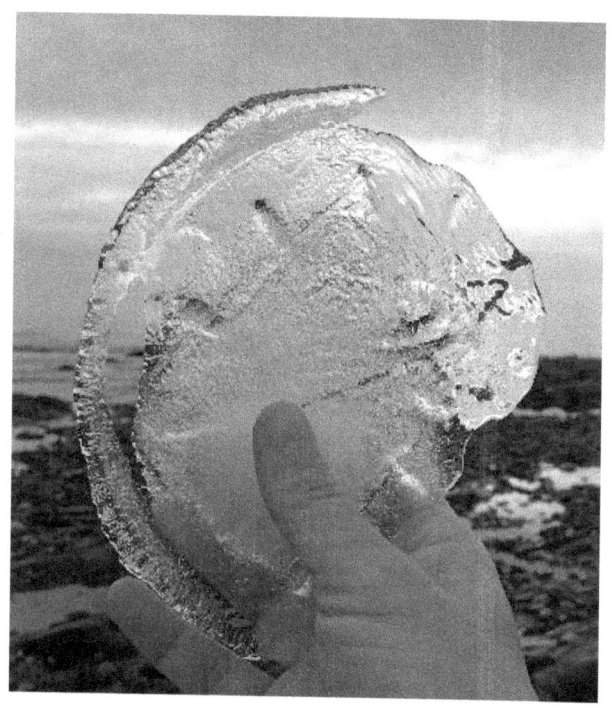

Fig. 2.1 – Guendalina Rota, 'Ongoing temporality', 2021

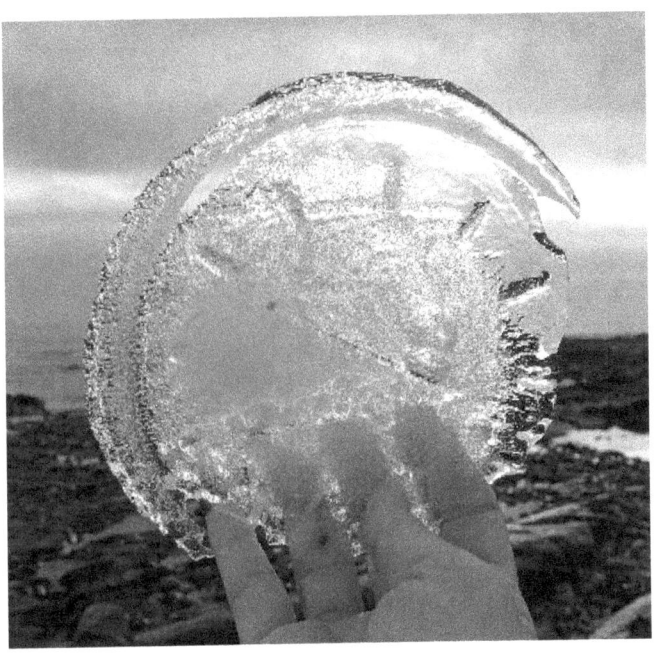

Fig. 2.2 - Guendalina Rota, 'Ongoing temporality', 2021

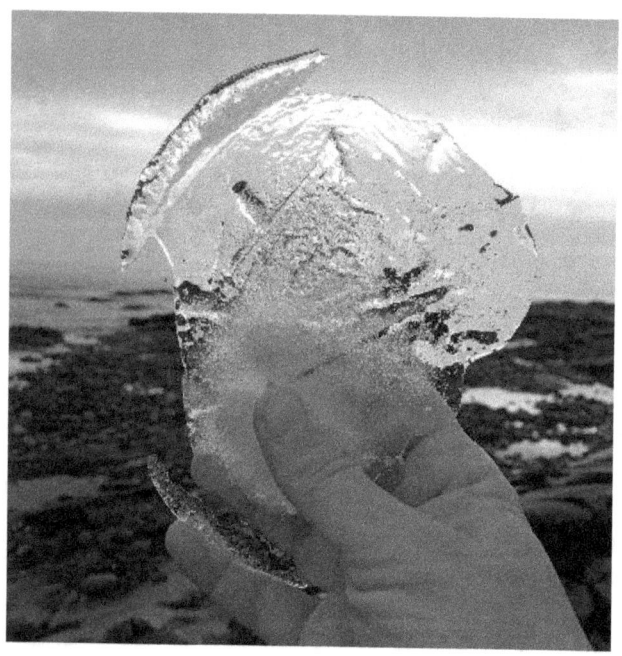

Fig. 2 3 - Guendalina Rota, 'Ongoing temporality', 2021

Calculative thinking and contemplative thinking

Following the idea that everything is uncertain and questionable, I return to Heidegger's claim that the only certain thing is death, and the only way to live an authentic life is by being aware that our life has an end, which pushes us to live better. And it is precisely in the speech for the celebration of the 175th birthday of the composer Conradin Kreutzer that Heidegger, through the composer's death, commemorates life, explaining how there are two types of thought and why we are unable to detach ourselves from objects, in particular technological ones, and as a result, we are unable to perceive the true meaning of the circumstances that arise, escaping what is an authentic life.

In his "Memorial address', Heidegger states that we recollect memories to celebrate someone's life, '...but at the bottom we merely allow ourselves to be entertained by such a talk." (Heidegger, 1966: 44). There is no thinking involved, we just absorb given notions.

> Thoughtlessness is an uncanny visitor who comes and goes everywhere in today's world. For nowadays we take in everything in the quickest and cheapest way, only to forget it just as quickly, instantly. (Heidegger,1966: 45)

He adds that one becomes deaf only when one can hear first, one gets old only if one is young first, in the same way one is thoughtless because one can think, and "man at the core of his being has the capacity to think: has 'spirit and reason' and is destined to think". (Heidegger, 1966: 45). The problem at bottom is the fact that man neither sees nor admits that he is "fleeing from thinking" (Heidegger, 1966: 45). Indeed, he very easily states the opposite, and with reason: there has never been before a knowledge that goes so far and reaches so many topics. But this is a kind of knowledge and thinking that is based on given conditions, the intrinsic nature of the given facts is not considered, "we take them into account with the calculated intention of their serving specific purposes." (Heidegger, 1966: 46), and this is a calculated thought that has predetermined objectives as its goal.

Waiting for a Title to Reveal Itself

If we pause to consider the historical context in which this discourse takes place, I am amazed at how the underlying concepts are extremely current. Is it not true that technology has overwhelmed us, bombarding us with news and notions that continually and assiduously enter our lives? We have access to an incredible amount of information in every possible field and it is within everyone's reach, at all ages. Our lives are constantly dependent on technological objects, and we are unable to give up their use. How many of us, leaving the house, if they realize that they do not have a mobile phone with them, do not hurry back?

This kind of calculative thinking that exists nowadays takes into consideration facts that are already there and are always on the move and never stops: "Calculative thinking races from one prospect to the next" (Heidegger, 1966, P46). Human beings always need a purpose, our actions have a purpose, and when a task is completed, we rush towards the next, without stopping. We are obsessed with going from A to B, our modern society urges us to hurry, to do and to have 'everything and now'. Slowness is seen as a weakness; a child is considered slow if he has learning difficulties; only those who arrive first are rewarded, we focus on the finish line without considering the path to get there. During this race, man loses sight of the intrinsic meaning of the facts that arise or of the objects he decides to use, as Heidegger explained in 'Being and Time', speaking of man as a potential for existence. Yet it is all around us, if only we could stop and notice it, but the true content of things often eludes us, as human beings stop and think less and less. With technology we do not need to verify, investigate, explore, a machine does not lie, and we accept and absorb notions in an anesthetized way, by hearsay, and this is not, perhaps, the inauthentic life that Heidegger spoke of in 'Being and time'?

I myself feel depending on my technological devices very much, and I surely have lots of information, every day, that passes under my eyes: I see but I do not see, I acknowledge their existence, but I do not stop to verify every single notion, it is very true that I take in consideration only the information that I need to pursue some project, or idea.

This is precisely my struggle: I always run, with a sense of exhaustion and discontent, but I feel empty at the end, and it is not the time that I must stop: it is I who needs to pause, it is I who decides my project of existence and, consequently, it is I who needs to change.

Heidegger does not judge or condemn this way of being, it simply is as it is. But he also says that 'There are, then, two kinds of thinking, each justified and needed in its own way: calculative thinking and meditative thinking.' (Heidegger, 1966: 46). He also says that man's true nature is 'to think meditatively 'because man is a thinking, that is, a meditating being' (Heidegger, 1966: 47), but then why we are no longer able to do it? Because it is easy to denigrate the meditative type of thinking as it does not conform to the demands of today's hectic life, it takes too much time, it does not produce goods or money, it has no set goals, it is too elitist, it is above and out of reach of ordinary people, and the list could go further. Therefore, we are 'in flight-from-thinking, [...]mere meditative thinking finds itself floating unaware above reality. It loses touch. It is worthless for dealing with current business. It profits nothing in carrying out practical affairs.' (Heidegger, 1966: 46).

In summary, we have seen that there are two types of thinking: calculating thinking and meditative thinking. For Heidegger, man is by nature a thinking being, but nowadays calculative thinking has taken over for a whole series of reasons, substantially linked to technology and capitalism, which continually push us to plan, organize and, consequently, make us stressed and alienated. Without contemplative thinking, we are unable to see the true nature of the world, and instead run the risk of considering it simply and only a great resource.

Releasement towards things and openness to the mystery

We have seen that there are many excuses for not using a meditative thought, but as I said, they are excuses, and we will see why. Yet one thing is true: although man, according to Heidegger, is naturally inclined to meditative thought, this remains out of the ordinary because it does not happen by itself but is the result of persistent training and sometimes can require a significant effort, in other words, it needs to be awakened. Heidegger himself states that it is not an easy task: 'At times it requires a greater effort. It demands more practice. It is in need of even more delicate care than any other genuine craft. But it must also be able to bide its time, to await as does the farmer, whether the seed will come up and ripen.' (Heidegger, 1966: 47).

We could argue that one of the reasons for being such a challenging task is the pervasive technology that continually assails us with information at such a rate that it is really difficult, if not impossible, to be able to verify everything. This leads us to prefer calculative thinking as it explores the usefulness of things without the desire or the effort to deepen knowledge of objects, considering the object just related to its purpose and not for what it is. As we saw earlier in this paper when I considered our relationship with things, the risk of thinking calculative is that our life becomes inauthentic, somehow, we lower ourselves by becoming objects ourselves, no longer thinking human beings.

The fact is, we are chained and enslaved by technology. It is essential, our life is linked to it and it is undoubtedly better in terms of efficiency and potential. 'It would be foolish to attack technology blindly [...] but suddenly and unaware we find ourselves so firmly shackled to these technical devices that we fall into bondage to them.' (Heidegger,1966: 54).

Heidegger suggests that the way to free us from this vicious circle and enslavement with technological objects is to use meditative thinking, 'It is enough if we dwell on what lies close and meditate on what is closest; upon that which concerns us, each one of us, here and now; here, on this patch of home grown; now, in the present hour of history' (Heidegger, 1966: 47). As we said before, man is fully capable of doing it but, somehow, he has forgotten about it. The human being must strive to be able to awaken this ability to think meditatively and to maintain a constant use of it so that it happens spontaneously. But why can this kind of thinking help us? Meditative thinking observes, evaluates, realizes what surrounds us, does not stop at hearsay but deepens. It does not take us away from reality as one of the critics would have us believe by saying that it floats above the world and objects but goes deep into the world and the objects themselves and in this way comes remarkably close to reality. 'Meditative thinking demands of us not to cling one-sidedly to a single idea, nor to run down a one-track course of ideas. Meditative thinking demands of us that we engage ourselves with what at first sight does not go together at all' (Heidegger, 1966: 53). The extreme focus of meditative thinking allows us to understand that we are chained to technological devices, awaken awareness in us and allowing free will. If we are aware do be addicted, we can choose to be free and use them only when we need. 'We can affirm the unavoidable use of technical devises, and deny them the right to dominate us, and so to warp, confuse, and lay waste our nature.' (Heidegger, 1966: 54). In a way it is like saying 'yes' and 'no' at the same time and this attitude, instead of being synonymous with insecurity, puts us in control of the situation with a relaxed attitude, and free, 'I would call this comportment [...] releasement toward things.' (Heidegger, 1966: 54). In other words, releasement towards things is the ability to let go of the desire to want to explain everything rationally, is a radical change in the way of thinking that allows us to understand the implicit and hidden meaning of things.

> If we explicitly and continuously heed the fact that such hidden meaning touches us everywhere in the world of technology, we stand at once within the realm of that which hides itself from us and hides itself just in approaching us. That which shows itself and at the same time withdraws is the essential trait of what we call the mystery. I call the comportment which enables us to keep open to the meaning hidden in technology, openness to the mystery. Releasement towards things and openness to the mystery belong together. (Heidegger, 1966: 55).

This concept is crucial in Heidegger's philosophy. In this case, the word 'releasement' is one of the translations from the German Gelassenheit, but not the best because it is a complex concept more than a simple verb or noun. We will see, as we proceed along this path, that this is one of the key points of Heidegger's philosophy and the concept that will open new horizons for me. A concept that will then be tackled along the work entitled 'Country path conversations' in a slow and profound way, without ever revealing itself completely, leaving the reader with the task of deciphering the intrinsic suggestions hidden through the pages and the possibility of learning the meditative thinking.

Gelassenheit.

Undoubtedly, 'Conversation in a country path' is a work that really resonates in my state of mind with his concept of Gelassenheit. In this book a scientist, a scholar and a guide meet along a country path and find themselves talking thickly, with the accent of someone who is sure of their truths and wants to convince others of them too. This, at least, for the scientist and the scholar. The guide personifies Heidegger's thinking, he intervenes with the same discretion as a narrator, without impositions, without judgments, but with questions and statements that make you think and, without instructions or explanations, leads both the scientist and the scholar to rethink their beliefs by opening doubts and showing the same things from a different point of view. And in this beautiful metaphor that is the country path, Heidegger reveals, or perhaps induces the reader to discover the meaning of Gelassenheit which, in my opinion, is one of the most complex and yet enlightening thinking on human being.

I would like to clarify that the concept of Gelassenheit is not easy to explain, and this is perhaps the reason why Heidegger never arrives at a precise statement but leaves clues, as if he wanted an active participation of the reader to whom he leaves the big task of understanding what it is. The previous chapters are in fact preparatory and support the full understanding of the meaning of Gelassenheit, as they already contain some fundamental thoughts that complete the picture of this state of being that is Gelassenheit.

The term Gelassenheit was first introduced by Meister Eckhart, medieval theologian, philosopher and mystic of the Dominican Order. With this term he has enriched the German language with a new vocable that, because of its complexity, cannot be translated with only one word but with a full whole concept. For Eckhart it is a detachment, releasement in a spiritual sense, it includes calm, adoration, humility, dedication to arrive at the final stage which is union with God.

Heidegger takes this term and make it its own, maintaining its complexity but taking distance from the idea of total devotion to any kind of divine will. The meaning of Gelassenheit in Eckart's Christianity meant a renunciation or abandonment of the will of oneself and a release of things entirely to the sole and full will of God. Heidegger states that release it is not within the power of the free will, it is a release that happens when, we are willing of non-willing. While this sounds like a paradox, it is exactly the right frame of mind to let the release into things and openness to mystery, that we have already considered, take place. Yes, because these two concepts are at the heart of Gelassenheit. This is a very difficult idea to understand and can lead to misunderstandings. The releasement is considered as non-willing, but the idea of non-willing should not be misunderstood as an active choice of refusal or lack of will, therefore remaining in the domain of the will. According to Heidegger, in order to allow, or enter, Gelassenheit we must be able to give up the will, this is the first step to allow an awakening in Gelassenheit. We must learn to let go of the calculative thought, which we have already encountered, renounce wanting to explain everything with reason, and learn a way of thinking that detaches itself from the will. The struggle in understanding this passage can be found in the conversation as well:

> 'Scholar: Yet thinking, conceived of the traditional manner as representing, is a willing; even Kant conceives of thinking in this manner when he characterizes it as spontaneity. Thinking is willing, and willing is thinking.
>
> Scientist: The assertion that the essence of thinking is something other than thinking,

then, says that thinking is something other than willing.

Guide: That is why, in answer to your question as to what I really will in our meditation on the essence of thinking, I replied: I will non-willing.' (Heidegger, 2016: 68)

In conversation the scholar and scientist cannot find a way to understand the essence of thought as liberation without the will to think.

The guide recognizes this struggle in the way of thinking itself, which hinders their way of opening up, and when asked what they should do, the guide responds: "we should do nothing at all, but rather wait" (Heidegger, 2016: 71)

Waiting is a fundamental point in understanding Gelassenheit. Heidegger argues that higher action takes the form of waiting. The ability to release the calculative thinking and, with it, the will, brings us closer to ourselves, to our essence and allows us to enter into ourselves, into our most authentic self, as we saw in 'Being and Time'. We enter into ourselves and into Gelassenheit, we open ourselves to our innermost self and we open ourselves to Gelassenheit. Our superior action, in this case, is not a practical action that contains a cause-effect but leads to the true essence of things.

In summary, we have said that waiting is a key point of Gelassenheit. But we must be careful not to ask ourselves what we are waiting for, because it would give us a purpose by making us fall back into calculative thinking. Heidegger, on purpose, never explains what Gelassenheit is because he wants to leave us open to the mystery, and the openness to the mystery keeps open the possibilities of being in Gelassenheit. Yes, because it is not a thing to explain, but rather a condition to live in, to learn, and it does not happen by itself, but we have to allow it to happen. It is no coincidence that a trio of people is chosen to discuss what Gelassenheit is in 'Country path conversation': the presence of three completely different points of view makes possible the oscillatory movement of thought that continually returns to itself when compared, it is never static, it opens up to new and unexpected paths, to a new space, to a new horizon that it is possibility, it is truth and meditative thinking is activated there.

According to the human being the horizon is an opening, it is not an object in itself but the space of our visual field, therefore in front of us, where the objects exist: more precisely, we can determine the horizon exclusively from the objects it contains, therefore it is a space defined by what is inside it, and we can perceive it because we use a representative thought, we need to represent those objects in our thinking in order to perceive the horizon. Heidegger says that the horizon is an open region and it is all around us, but we cannot recognize it or realize its presence because our representative thinking keeps us anchored in our visual field. If we manage to release ourselves from representative thinking, the objects can lose their function and return to their essence of origins, where they simply exist, detached from the idea of space and time and in their true self. We ourselves return to the origin, to our Da-sein, to our true nature as meditative thinker in a timeless space, where we simply wait. In this waiting the horizon reveal itself: this region, that Heidegger calls Gegnet, come to meet and open itself to us. In other words, if we could welcome the things around us without giving them any purpose for our life potential, those things would no longer be just our projection of them but could reveal their authentic self. We would lose our calculative thinking and, without expectations and projects, we could wait for the Gegnet to come to us. We are in it, in this openness we are in Gelassenheit, that is around us and has always been. 'The essence of this waiting is, however, releasement to the open-region. Yet because it is the open-region which now and again lets releasement belong to itself, the essence of thinking rest in the fact that, if I may say so, the open-region enregions releasement in itself.' (Heidegger, 2016: 79).

Water

'Human eye cannot see

the incessant caress of the water on rocks

but his hand will reach the pebble

and a whiff of eternity

will touch his soul.'

Guendalina Rota, 'Caress', 2021.

In this chapter I hope, with a brief list of examples, just outlined and, somehow, as elusive as water, to arouse curiosity, to engage a desire for exploration, to highlight the common points between the Heideggerian

Dasein and a more contemporary reflection on existence, finding ourselves within Gelassenheit, with our edges smoothed like pebbles, following this flow by activating our personal research. I would like to clarify that I have deliberately chosen to describe the examples below only superficially because the function of these pieces is to stimulate inquisitiveness, to leave interpretative freedom to the reader who can thus find its way from a personal point of view.

With the performance 'Being water', I come out of my being, trying to understand how the water works and, imitating its slow flow on the stones, my fingers slide on the clay smoothing it, levelling it, in a repetition of caresses in slow motion: I become water. There is no calculative thinking behind the action of making pebbles, my purpose is not a specific final number of pieces but the process itself, and I release myself to this action without a goal in mind but following the course of the action in complete openness for what is to come. This is how I find myself among those pebbles, those concepts shaped by Heidegger's Philosophy, simply waiting.

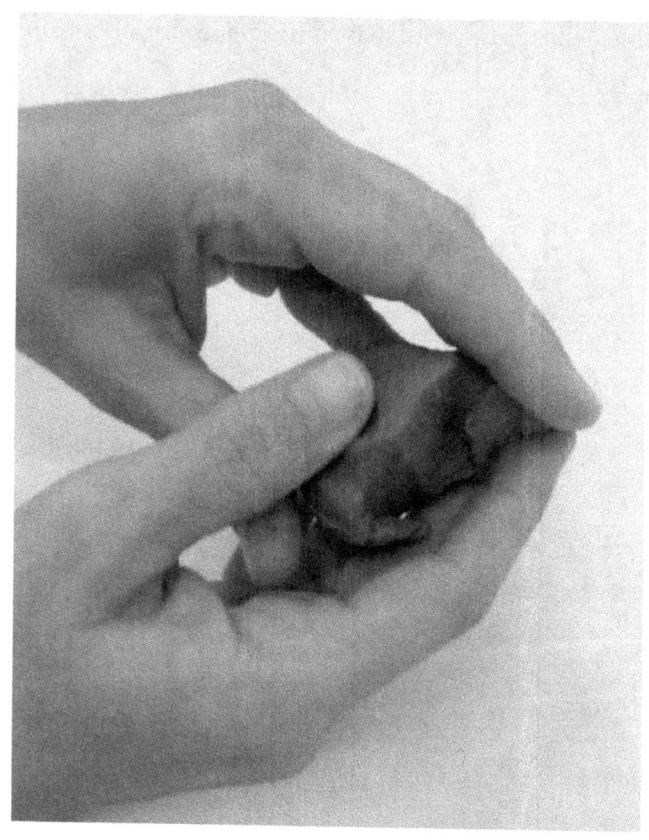

Fig. 3.1 - Guendalina Rota, 'Being water', 2021

Waiting for a Title to Reveal Itself

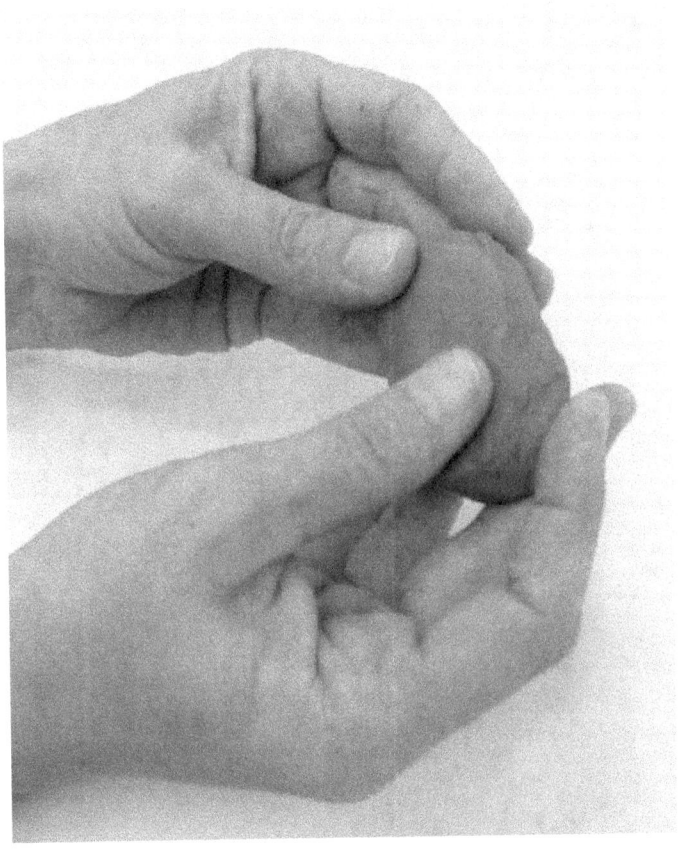

Fig. 3.2 - Guendalina Rota, 'Being water', 2021

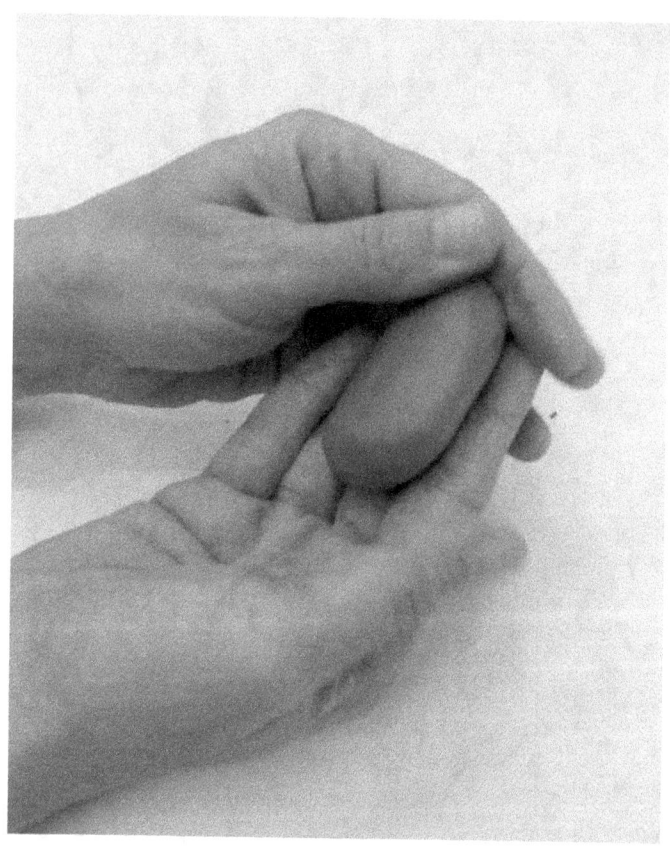

Fig. 3.3 - Guendalina Rota, 'Being water', 2021

Wonder for the sake of wonder

While I wait, I happen to encounter Erling Kagge's 'Silence in the Age of Noise'. Similarly to Heidegger, I can see the exploration of a human being that is trying to be Dasein, aware to exist there at that particular moment in time. With a series of examples, of which an expedition to Antarctica is the starting point, Kagge explains how, with silence, it is possible to detach from the hectic modern life, without judging it, without denying it, but simply by taking time and space to be able to regenerate ourselves in a sort of metaphorical cocoon, where we can transcend from what surrounds us. 'In a way, silence […] It's about getting inside what you are doing. Experiencing rather than over-thinking. Allowing each moment to be big enough. Not living through other people and other things.' (Kagge, 2017: 51).

In this book, he explains how to create the perfect environment, the necessary silence, while remaining physically in the world. 'I was consumed by all that I saw and I shut out the noise. You cannot wait for it to get quiet.

Not in New York, not anywhere else. You must create your own silence.' (Kagge, 2017: 57).

I think that we can be Dasein within the 'silence'. Is this not, perhaps, the idea of waiting within the horizon? 'Is it possible to both be present in the world and not present at the same time? [...] Time suddenly stops and I am simultaneously inwardly present and completely distant.' (Kagge, 2017: 96).

I would argue that an analogous experience happened during the piece 'The artist is present', by Marina Abramović. In this performance, Marina is seated at a relatively small table and the audience, in turn, is invited to sit in front of her in silence and as long as they wish. Marina is motionless, waiting, open to what will come, which in this case is the next participant, not knowing what he will bring her, yet in her openness she reaches the hidden and most intimate aspect of the person in front of her. In general, we could say that Marina, in her performative work, is like the guide in 'Country path talk', and instead of confronting the thoughts of a scientist and a scholar, she uses silence and her body as tools to guide the public to reflect and meditate.

The art of lingering

I glimpse Heidegger's philosophy also in Byung-Chul Han's 'The Scent of Time' which, trying to reflect on modern times, recognizes how technology has pushed us to increase the rhythms of our life, making us completely lose synchronicity with the bigger picture that is the world. We do not value the waiting anymore, the path taken to reach certain goals is not considered, because we live in an age where things happen here and now, where the purpose of technology is to make everything available in a click, therefore we focus only on the final achievement. 'The totalization of the Here removes the There. [...] Any There disappears in a side-by-side of events, sensations and information that has no gasp. Everything is Here. The There is no longer of any importance.' (Han, 2017b: 38).

We have seen how Heidegger views technology as the cause of our inability to think meditatively and how, regarding the concept of existence, the human being is considered Dasein, being There. If we remove the 'There', what kind of existence do we have left? If the time 'in between' disappears, we lose our history, we do not have memories, identities. 'If things are deprived of memory, they become information or commodities. They are pushed into a time-free, ahistorical space. The storage of information is preceded by the deletion of memory, the deletion of historical time.' (Han, 2017: 6). Is this not, perhaps, an example of what Heidegger considered to become an object and therefore to have an inauthentic life? And where Heidegger says that meditative thinking is the solution to living an authentic existence, Han suggests rediscovering the art of lingering.

'Life dominated by work is a *vita activa* which is entirely cut off from the *vita contemplativa*. If the human being loses all capacity for contemplation, it degenerates into an *animal labourans*.' (Han, 2017: 92). We can see animal labourans as calculative thinking. 'Active life [...] uses up time. [...] Things are destroyed and time is killed. Contemplative lingering gives time. It widens that being that is more than being-active. When life regains its capacity for contemplation, it gains in time and space, in duration and vastness.' (Han, 2017: 113).

Basia Irland, with her piece 'Contemplation Station', understands the need to disconnect from the hectic life and the need to take a break, a break that allows us to think, meditate, sit alone and be able to appreciate more deeply the things around us, like the song of a bird or the murmur of water.

In the same way, Louise Scullion and Matthew Dalziel, with the Rosnes Bench, offer a special place that allows people to lay down and rediscover the art of lingering.

The same need is fulfilled within the Roden Crater by James Turrell, a structure that combines art, astronomy, physics, technology, ancient history by isolating and intensifying the light of the celestial bodies in an unprecedented scenario. In an analogous way, Wolfang Laib and the wax room offer an enclosed space where you can detach yourself from the world and, somehow, find a way for meditative thinking.

I would argue that, even only on an unconscious level, these artists and writers retrace Heidegger's thoughts, making them their own, reconnecting with Gelassenheit, detaching themselves from the stressful rhythms of modern life, learning again to meditate as a response to the need for something that is missing, even if it is not clear what it is. Their words and art resonate perfectly with my feelings.

Time

As I said at the beginning of this paper, mine is the desire to be able to understand the reason for my constant sense of incompleteness. I have always felt the urge to change the pace of my life, which is too hectic, and I have always attributed the inability to do so to the chronic lack of time.

But that is not it.

Reading Heidegger and after encountering the concept of Gelassenheit, I realized that my existence leaves room only for a calculating thought, while I need to sit, not at the edge of the horizon but within it, letting go of all my wills and opening up. To myself.

So I will wait.

Yes, of course, time is involved here, but it is not counted, measured because I do not know how long I will wait, I do not know what I am waiting for, it is a wait on myself, I wait without expecting anything.

And the feeling of having no expectations is pure freedom.

I wait and I am at peace.

I just wait.

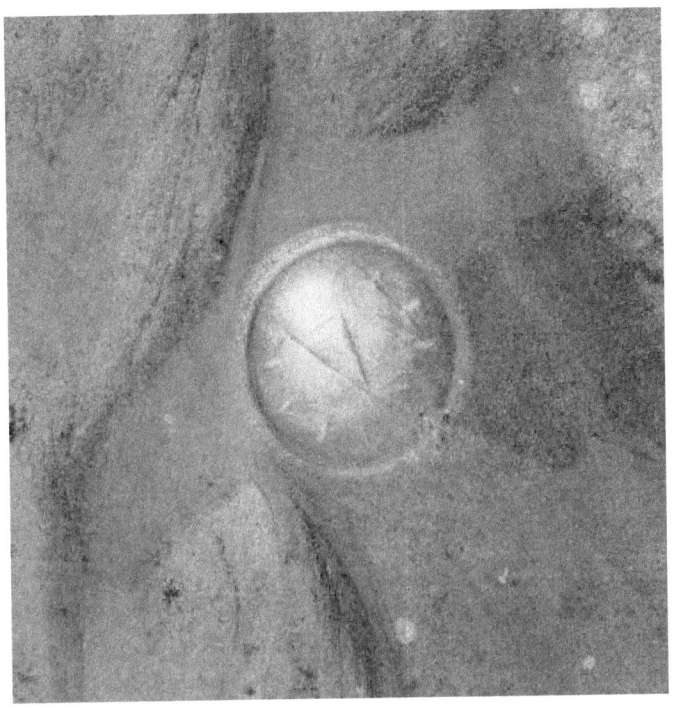

Fig. 4. Guendalina Rota, 'I will tell you when the time come', 2021

Waiting for a Title to Reveal Itself

While waiting...

'To see a World in a Grain of Sand
And a Heaven in a Wild Flower,
Hold Infinity in the palm of your hand
And Eternity in an hour.'

William Blake, *Auguries of Innocence*, 1803

Guendalina Rota

Bibliography

References:

Han B.-C. (2017) *The scient of time,* translated by Daniel Steuer (Polity Press, Cambridge, UK).

Heidegger M. (1962) *Being and Time,* translated by John Macquarrie & Edward Robinson (Blackwell Publishers Ldt, Oxford, Uk).

Heidegger M. (1966) *Discourse on Thinking,* translated by John M. Anderson and Hans Freund (Harper & Row, Publishers, New York, USA).

Heidegger M. (2016) *Country Path Conversations,* translated by Bret W. Davis (Indiana University Press, Bloomington, Indiana, USA).

Kagge E. (2017) *Silence in the age of noise,* translated by Becky L. Crook (Penguin Random House, UK).

Visual references:

Fig. 1 - Guendalina Rota, The gift, pencil, fine liner and ink, 2021. Photograph taken by me.

Fig. 2 - Guendalina Rota, 'Ongoing temporality', triptych. Sculpture made of ice, held until melted completely, 2021. Photographs taken by me.

Fig. 3 - Guendalina Rota, act of making pebbles, screenshot from a short documentary 'Being water', 2021. Photographs taken by me.

Fig. 4 - Guendalina Rota, I will tell you when the time comes, ice and rock, 2021, Photograph taken by me.

Sources consulted:

Babich, B. (2017) *Heidegger on technology and Gelassenheit: wabi-sabi and the art of Verfallenheit . AI & Soc* 32, 157–

166. https://doi.org/10.1007/s00146-015-0605-8, (accessed 26/12/2021).

D'Agnese V. (2015) *Progetto e possibilità in Heidegger: la radicale apertura dell'educazione come sfida al nichilismo.* Metisjournal.it, anno V – Numero 1 – 06/2015 L'educazione ai tempi della crisi. http://www.metisjournal.it/metis/anno-v-numero-1-062015-leducazione-ai-tempi-della-crisi/128-saggi/708-progetto-e-possibilita-in-heidegger-la-radicale-apertura-delleducazione-come-sfida-al-nichilismo.html (Accessed 28/12/2021).

Dalle Pezze B. (2006) *Heidegger on Gelassenheit.* ISSN 1393-614X *Minerva - An Internet Journal of Philosophy* Vol. 10 2006. http://www.minerva.mic.ul.ie/vol10/Heidegger.html (Accessed 21/12/2021).

Erickson, S. A. (1991). The Relevance of Meditative Thinking. *The Journal of Speculative Philosophy*, *5*(1),

25–41. http://www.jstor.org/stable/25669982 (Accessed 31/12/2021)

O'Leary J.S. (2014) Everyday Life and Ultimate Reality: Dialectical Reversals in Hegel, Heidegger and Buddhism, Contemporary Buddhism, 15:2, 465-478, DOI: 10.1080/14639947.2014.936654 (Accessed 28/11/2021)

Rae G. (2014) Transforming Thought: Heidegger and Meditative Thinking. In: Ontology in Heidegger and Deleuze. Palgrave Macmillan, London. https://doi.org/10.1057/9781137404565_5 (Accessed 30/12/2021)

Schrag C.O. (1970) *Heidegger on Repetition and Historical Understanding.* Philosophy East and West, Jul.1970, Vol. 20, No. 3 (Jul. 1970), pp. 287-295 Published by: University of Hawai'i Press, stable URL: https://www.jstor.org/stable/1398310 (Accessed 29/12/2021).

Schürmann, R. (1973). Heidegger and Meister Eckhart on Releasement. *Research in Phenomenology*, *3*, 95–119.

http://www.jstor.org/stable/24654259 (Accessed 17/12/2021).

Vallega-Neu, D. (2015). Heidegger's Reticence: From Contributions to Das Ereignis and toward Gelassenheit. *Research in Phenomenology* 45, 1, 1-32, Available From: Brill https://doi.org/10.1163/15691640-12341300 [Accessed 28/12/2021]

Author biography

An award-winning graduate in Fine Arts and Philosophy, Guendalina questions modern values and priorities by offering an alternative point of view, with a nod to phenomenology, suggesting that our ancestral relationship with nature could be the key.

Acknowledgements

I would like to express my deep gratitude to my supervisor, Dr. Tina Röck who, with cunning and delicacy, took me by the hand, listened to me thoroughly, believed in me and respected my times, making me understand that the subject of my dissertation was waiting for me, within myself. Thank you Tina, you have always been there for me and I feel lucky to have had the opportunity to work with you: your knowledge and passion have been truly inspiring. I would also like to thank the whole department of Art and Philosophy, in particular Dr. Undine Sellbach and Dr. Dominic Smith, who have accompanied me for four years on this path, finding the right words when I felt I was not enough. To Philip Braham for having been so patient in waiting to read my draft and for always being available, even during the Christmas holidays. A special thank goes to Dr. Helen Gørrill and Boom Graduates for publishing my dissertation and for the incredible energy and enthusiasm shown, even before meeting me in person, making me feel very special. Helen, your warmth is contagious and very much needed in this world. To my family who respected my need to be alone while I was working and who, without asking, looked after me while writing the dissertation. Last but not least, I would like to thank my former lecturer Alex Harvey, who has never stopped, not even for a second, to believe in me and who continues to follow me in all my achievements. Alex you are one of a kind and I feel blessed to have met you in my journey.

Boom!

This book was originally submitted as a dissertation in partial fulfilment of the requirements of a Bachelor of Arts (Hons) degree in Fine Art and Philosophy at the Duncan of Jordanstone College of Art and Design, the University of Dundee, in 2022.

Guendalina Rota

A note about Boom Graduates

We propel graduates forward so they can make their mark on the world - we push the boundaries, share brilliant ideas and inspire possibility. We publish dissertations as books, presented gift-boxed at graduation ceremonies, delivering brand-new research to the world quicker than anyone else. We plant trees for every commissioned book sold, and give our Boom graduates the chance to profit-share from their brilliant ideas. Furthermore we donate the majority of our profits to funding research and scholarship for disadvantaged students who wouldn't normally be able to attend university. Through academic excellence and environmental sustainability, *Boom Graduates* are changing the world.

We are Boom Graduates - an imprint of Boom Publications Ltd. We are a more-than-profit company, dedicating over half our profits to providing university scholarships for underprivileged students across the world. We aim to become the globe's biggest provider of such scholarships – and if like Guendalina, the author of this book, you'd also like to contribute to making the world a better place, please contact us: we publish monographs, edited books, and moreover our graduate series – Boom Graduates – are presented at graduation days across the world in archival, lined museum-quality presentation cases, engraved with the graduate's name and award.

Boom Publications are based at the Duncan of Jordanstone College of Art and Design, at the University of Dundee in Scotland. We were one of the winners of the 2022 Venture awards hosted by the Centre for Entrepreneurship, and have since been shortlisted for the Converge Challenge, a national award that brings together ambitious and creative thinkers with innovative ideas to work with industry experts to transform their ideas into sustainable companies operating in the commercial world. We are also climate conscious and work with agencies to plant a tree for each and every book commissioned, offsetting thousands of tonnes of carbon each year. Follow us on social media to watch our forest grow @boomgraduates.

Thank you for contributing by purchasing this book. Please visit our catalogues on www.boompublications.com.

Guendalina Rota

Notes

Guendalina Rota

Waiting for a Title to Reveal Itself

Waiting for a Title to Reveal Itself

Guendalina Rota

Waiting for a Title to Reveal Itself

Guendalina Rota

Waiting for a Title to Reveal Itself

Guendalina Rota

Waiting for a Title to Reveal Itself

www.ingramcontent.com/pod-product-compliance
Lightning Source LLC
Chambersburg PA
CBHW070253220526
45465CB00004B/1610